C000118990

Learn French with Anaïs

As if you were having private lessons

For intermediates

Volume 2

Preface

During the past five years of my teaching French, I had the opportunity to create my own teaching materials which follow a logical progression in learning the language. As my experience in learning English at school wasn't great, I decided to focus on creating an enjoyable way of learning French through dynamic, fun and rewarding lessons.

I am often asked, "do you have a good book to recommend to French learners?" It an undeniable fact that there are so many books available today for French learners. They all have their advantages and disadvantages, but they are often written in the same way. This is why I have decided to write a series of books believing that it will help a few learners by giving them a different approach.

This book is not your usual study guide; it offers a different way to learn French and a different approach to self-teaching. It may not be the best book out there, and this is not the intention. However, the book is based on my experience in teaching French to people of intermediate level. It follows the teaching method I have been using for years.

With this book, you can teach yourself French with or without having private French lessons. It will help you avoid picking up bad habits, as can commonly happen when you learn a new language on your own.

You can enjoy yourself while learning French with this well-made book. It is easy to read, clear and easy to understand. The lessons have been put in a special order, mixing grammar, tenses, vocabulary, and verbs, to make way for clear progression and effective learning. I recommend that you learn the lessons the way they are presented. You will find lessons made by points with short explanations and examples.

Everything in this book is designed to help the learner keep their motivation at a high level. Motivation is really important to learn a new language and having goals to achieve along the way will help you.

Setting a time for French is a good idea, and with this book, you can learn at your own pace. The "lessons" can fit your schedule as you decide when and for how long you want to study.

This book allows you to learn French as if you were having private French lessons, so you could choose to do one hour a week of French or perhaps thirty minutes a day.

No matter how long you decide to study per week, it is important to choose a realistic and achievable goal. If you have a busy schedule, planning to do one hour a day, for example, isn't achievable and will demotivate you.

Using an exercise book could help you maintain your motivation. You can boost your progress with the exercises book called "Learn French with Anaïs, intermediates' exercises book," test yourself and monitor your progress. The exercise book contains exercises specially made for you to practice the grammar points, the verbs, the tenses and the vocabulary you find in this book. It is a good book to use alongside this one.

This book is the fourth of a series. You can purchase the beginners' volumes 1 and 2 to help you refresh the basics, the present tense and more, as well as the exercise books that go with it. The intermediates volume 1 is also available and will help you master the different past tenses and more. The advanced level will follow, as well as the advanced exercise books; so, watch out for them.

Table des matières
Table of contents

Lexique grammatical
Glossary of grammar terms

Adjective

It's a word that describes or tells more about something or someone such as their size, colour, qualities…

e.g., Tall, blue, big, happy…

Adverb

It's a word that gives more information about how, when, where, in what circumstances something happened.

e.g., Quickly, happily, now…

Agree/Agreement

It means that you have to change the endings of the words to show whether you are referring to feminine, masculine, singular or plural of people or things.

Article

It's a word used in front of nouns to give information about the gender and the quantity.

e.g., The, a, an, some ...

Auxiliary verb

It's a verb used to form compound tenses.

e.g., To be, to have.

Comparative

The comparative is used to compare differences between two things.

e.g., Taller than.

Consonant

It's a letter from the alphabet which is not a vowel.

e.g., C, d, f...

Conjugated

It's a verb with an ending based on the subject and the tense you are referring to.

e.g., I do.

Demonstrative pronoun

It's a pronoun used to point to specific things while speaking or describing.

e.g., This.

Direct object pronoun

It's a pronoun used to replace a group of words answering the question "who" for a person and "what" for an object.

Disjunctive pronoun

It's a pronoun used to emphasize a noun or a pronoun that refers to a person.

e.g., Me, you ...

Ending

It's what we add to a verb, an adjective or a noun depending on whether they refer to feminine, masculine, singular or plural.

e.g., She goes.

Feminine

It's a form of a noun, adjective or pronoun used to refer to a living being, thing or idea that is classed as feminine.

Gender

It's whether a noun, pronoun or adjective is feminine or masculine.

Indefinite pronoun

It's a pronoun used to refer to non-specific beings, objects, or places.

e.g., Anyone

Indirect object pronoun

It's a pronoun used to replace a group of words answering the question "to who" for a person and "to what" for an object.

Infinitive

It's the form of the verb with "to" in front of it, and without any endings added.

e.g., To walk.

Invariable

It means that it doesn't change.

Irregular verb

It's a verb whose forms do not follow a regular pattern or a regular rule.

Locution

It's a group of words that have the same value as a single word.

e.g., Par exemple.

Masculine

It's a form of a noun, adjective or pronoun used to refer to a living being, thing or idea that is classed as masculine.

Modal verb

It's a verb that is usually used with another verb to express ideas such as possibility, necessity, and permission.

e.g., Can, should…

Negative

It's a question or a statement containing a word such as not, never or nothing.

e.g., I never eat cheese.

Noun

It's a naming word for a living being, a thing or idea.

e.g., A woman.

Plural

It's a form of a word used to refer to something that is more than one.

e.g., Tomatoes.

Possessive adjective

It's an adjective which shows who or what something belongs to or is connected with.

e.g., My, your …

Possessive pronoun

It's a pronoun used to indicate a possession.

e.g., Mine, yours …

Preposition

It's a word usually followed by a noun, a pronoun, or a verb in "-ing" in English.

e.g., At, to, in ...

Pronominal verb

It's a verb whose direct object is the same as its subject. A reflexive pronoun precedes it.

e.g., I bathe (myself).

Pronoun

It's a word used instead of a noun when you don't want to mention the name of something or someone directly or want to refer back to someone or something.

e.g., I want it.

Proper noun

It's a name used for a person, place, or organisation, spelled with an initial capital letter.

e.g., Paul.

Question word

It's a word used to ask a question.

e.g., Why, when …

Reciprocal

When the subject and the object of a sentence are mutually affected by the action, the sentence is said to be reciprocal.

e.g., Paul and I are meeting each other.

Reflexive

A sentence is said to be reflexive when the subject doing the action is also affected by the action.

e.g., I wake up. (myself)

Reflexive pronoun

It's a pronoun that will refer back to the person doing the action. It is used with reflexive verbs only.

e.g., Je me, tu te …

Regular verb

It's a verb whose forms follow a regular pattern or a regular rule.

Relative pronoun

It's a pronoun used to introduce relative clauses.

e.g., Who.

Singular

It's a form of a word used to refer to one person or thing.

e.g., A tomato.

Stem

It's the main part of the verb to which endings are added.

e.g., Play.

Subject

It's the noun in a sentence that refers to the person or the thing that does the action described by the verb.

e.g., My cat drinks.

Subject pronoun

It's a pronoun used instead of a noun as the subject of a sentence.

e.g., He, she, they ...

Superlative

The superlative is the highest or the lowest level of a comparative.

e.g., The biggest.

Tense

It's the form of a verb which shows whether you are referring to the present, past or future.

Verb

It's a "doing" word describing what someone or something does or is …

e.g., Be.

Vowel

It's a letter from the alphabet which is not a consonant.

e.g., A, e, i, o, u, y.

Prononciation des consonnes
Pronunciation of consonants

B = "b"
Bébé

L/ ll = "l"
Laura / Appelle

C = "k"
Carte

M/ mm = "m"
Maman / Pomme

D = "d"
Dinosaure

N/ nn = "n"
Non / Année

F = "f"
France

P/ pp = "p"
Poire / Appelle

G = "g"
Galaxie

Q = "k"
Qatar

H = silent
Hotel

R/ rr = "r"
Raisin / Verre

J = "j"
Jeudi

S/ss = "s"
Soleil / Basse

K = "k"
Koala

T = "t"
Thé

<u>V = "v"</u>
Venus

<u>X = "x"</u>
Xylophone

<u>W = "v"</u>
Wagon

<u>Z = "z"</u>
Zèbre

La prononciation des voyelles
Pronunciation of vowels

A = "ah"
Abracadabra

À/ â= "ah"
À / Âge

E = "uh"
Heure

Ë = "uh"
Noël "no-el"

I = "ee"
Italie

î= "ee"
Île

Ï = "ee"
Maïs "ma-iss"

O = "oh"
Octobre

Ô = "oh"
Côté

U = "ooh"
Tu

Ü= "ooh"
Müller

Y = "ee" / "yuh"
Xylophone / Yankee

Note: You find this sound in the English word "us."

La combinaison de lettres
Combination of letters

Er/ et/ ei/ ez/ ey/ ai/ aî/ ay/ é/ è/ ê = "ey"

Manger

Muet

Reine

Hockey

Allez

Maison

Désolé

Après

Même

En/ em/ ent/ an/ ant = "on"

Entrer

Embrasser

Sentiment

Angleterre

Maintenant

In/ im/ ain/ aim/ ein/ en = "ahn"

Vin

Impatient

Pain

Faim

Peinture

Lycéen

Au/ aux/ eau/ eaux = "oh"

Jaune

Chevaux

Gâteau

Gâteaux

Ou/ où/ oû = "oo"

Mouche

Où

Août

Oi/ oî/ oy = "wa"

Mois

Boîte

Voyage

Eu / eux / oeu = "uh"

Heureux

Soeur

Fleur

Ce/ se/ ç = "sss"

Face

Semaine

Garçon

Qu = "k"
Question
Qualité

On/ om = "ohn"
Citron
Nom

Ci / ti = "see"
Citron
Patience

Ui/ oui = "wee"
Huit
Oui

Un/ um = "uhn"
Lundi
Parfum

Ti = "tea"
Fatigue

Ch = " k"
Orchestre

Ch = "sh"
Cheval

Ail = "eye"
Bétail

Lle = "yuh"
Famille

Eil = "a" (English pronunciation)
Vieil

Oin = "wahn"
Foin

Gui = "gwee"
Aiguille

Gui = "ghee"
Guide

Gue = "geuh"
Fatigue

Gua = "gwa"
Iguane

Ge = "zh"
Mariage

Qua = "kwa"
Aquarium

Qui = "kwee"
Équilatéral

Ph = "f"
Pharmacie

Ps = "psss"
Psychologue

Gn = "nee-yuh"
Gagner

Th = "t"
Thé

Sc = "sk"
Score

Es = "eyss"
Esprit

Les lettres muettes et les liens
Silent letters and links

Letter omissions

We don't pronounce "s," "c," "t," "x," "d," "p," "f," "l," "g," and "z" when they are the last letter(s) of a word. But there are exceptions.

e.g., Oeufs
    Trop
    Sang
    Riz
    Chocolat
    Banc
    Pied
    Melons
    Heureux
    Gentil

We will pronounce "s," "c," "t," "d," "p," "f," "l," and "g" when an "e follows them." The "e" is silent, but there are exceptions. If the letters are followed by an "é" or an "è," it is not silent.

e.g., Verte
    Grande
    Parlé

Links

When a consonant follows a vowel or an "h," we link the consonant with the vowel. There are exceptions.

e.g., Mon petit (t)ami.

When "les," "des," "nous," "vous," "ils," or "elles" are followed by a word starting with a vowel or an "h," we use a "z" link.

e.g., Vous vous (z)appelez paul.

> *Note: Links are here to avoid going down (sloping) in the middle of a sentence because it is not something native French speakers do. As a result, sometimes links are not needed.*

Silent or aspirated "h"?

The silent "h"
The "h" will be silent when the article in front of it is "l'." In this case, we consider the "h" to be silent, and we use the "z" link with "des" or "les."

e.g., L'hôtel → Les (z)hôtels.

The aspirated "h"
The "h" will be aspirated when the article in front of it is "le" or "la." The "h" isn't silent and we can't link it with "des" or "les."

e.g., Le haricot → Les haricots.

S or z sound?

"Z" sound
When there is one "s" between two vowels, it sounds like a "z."

e.g., Hésiter → To hesitate "ey-zee-tey."

"S" sound
When there are two "s" between two vowels, they sound like an "s."

e.g., Assez → Enough "ah-sey."

L'alphabet
The alphabet

A	"ah"
B	"bey"
C	"sey"
D	"dey"
E	"uh"
F	"ef"
G	"jay"
H	"ash"
I	"ee"
J	"gee"
K	"kah"
L	"el"
M	"em"
N	"en"
O	"oh"
P	"pey"
Q	"kew"
R	"air"
S	"es"
T	"tey"

U	"ew"
V	"vey"
W	"doobluh vay"
X	"eeks"
Y	"ee-grek"
Z	"zed"

Note: Knowing the alphabet helps with pronunciation and is good for spelling of names and words.

Note: The French vowels are A, E, I, O, U and Y. "Y" is pronounced the same as "I."

Les moyens de paiement
The means of payments

De l'argent	Some money
Un euro	One euro
Un centime	One penny /A cent
Une pièce de monnaie	A coin
Un billet	A note
La monnaie	The change
Un chèque	A cheque
Un carnet de chèques	A chequebook
Une carte bleue	A debit /credit card
Une carte bancaire	A debit /credit card
Payer en espèce	To pay in cash
Payer par carte	To pay by card
Payer par chèque	To pay by cheque
Une machine à cartes	A card machine
Un distributeur automatique	An ATM
Un virement bancaire	A bank transfer
Un chèque cadeau	A gift voucher
Une carte cadeau	A gift card
Un bon de réduction	A discount voucher
Un remboursement	A refund
Un compte bancaire	A bank account
Une dette	A debt

La formation des adverbes
The formation of adverbs

What is it?

An adverb is an invariable word or a phrase that modifies the meaning of a verb, an adjective or another adverb.

What are they for?

The adverbs specify the circumstances of time, place or manner in which the action is happening. They can also indicate the degree of a quality or defect and can provide information on what the speaker thinks.

Adverbs ending in "-ment"

With feminine adjectives
Some adverbs are formed by adding "-ment" to the feminine adjective.

e.g., Claire → Clairement → Clearly.
     Douce → Doucement → Softly.

With masculine adjectives
Some adverbs are formed by adding "-ment" to the masculine adjective.

e.g., Joli → Joliment → Prettily.
     Vrai → Vraiment → Truly.

With adjectives ending in "e"
Some adjectives ending in a mute "e" change the "e" to an "é" before adding "-ment" to form the adverb.

e.g., Commun → Commune → Communément → Commonly.
     Énorme → Énorme → Énormément → Enormously.

With adjectives ending in "u"

Some masculine adjectives ending in "u" change the "u" to an "û" before adding "-ment" to form the adverb.

e.g., Continu → Continûment → Continually.
    Assidu → Assidûment → Attentively.

Adverbs ending in "-emment"

The adjectives ending in "-ent" form their adverbs in "-emment."

e.g., Prudent → Prudemment → Carefully.
    Impatient → Impatiemment → Impatiently.

Adverbs ending in "-amment"

The adjectives ending in "-ant" form their adverbs in "-amment."

e.g., Savant → Savamment → Cleverly.
    Bruyant → Bruyamment → Noisily.

Simple words

Some adverbs are not formed from an adjective, but they are just simple words.

e.g., Hier → Yesterday.
    Ici → Here.
    Maintenant → Now.

Group of words

A group of words forms some adverbs.

e.g., Tout à coup → Suddenly.
    Jusque-là → Until then.

Irregular adverbs

Adjective	Adverb	English
Bref	Brièvement	Briefly
Gentil	Gentiment	Nicely
Bon	Bien	Well / Good
Mauvais	Mal	Badly
Meilleur	Mieux	Better
Moindre	Moins	Less
Petit	Peu	Little
Lent	Lentement	Slowly

Adverbs identical to the masculine singular adjective

French	English
Bas	Low
Bon	Good
Chaud	Hot
Cher	Expensive
Clair	Clear
Court	Short
Dur	Hard
Faux	False
Fort	Loud / Strong
Mauvais	Bad

Les différents types adverbes
The different types of adverbs

Adverbs of places

Ailleurs	Elsewhere
Autour	Around
Avant	Before
Dedans	In / Inside
Dehors	Out / Outside
Derrière	Behind
Dessous	Under
Dessus	On
Devant	In front of
Ici	Here
Là	There
Loin	Far
Près	Close
Partout	Everywhere

Adverbs of time

Alors	Then
Après	After
Après-demain	The day after tomorrow
Aujourd'hui	Today
Aussitôt	Immediately
Avant	Before

Avant-hier	The day after yesterday
Bientôt	Soon
Déjà	Already
Demain	Tomorrow
Depuis	Since
Encore	Yet
Enfin	Finally
Ensuite	Then
Hier	Yesterday
Jamais	Never
Longtemps	Longtime
Maintenant	Now
Parfois	Sometimes
Puis	Then
Quelquefois	Sometimes
Soudain	Suddenly
Souvent	Often
Tard	Late
Tôt	Early
Toujours	Always

Adverbs of manner

Ainsi	Thereby / In this way
Bien	Well / Good
Comme	As
Debout	Up

Ensemble	Together
Exprès	On purpose
Mal	Bad
Mieux	Better
Plutôt	Rather
Vite	Fast / Quickly

Adverbs of quantity

Assez	Enough
Aussi	Also
Autant	As many … as
Beaucoup	A lot
Moins	Less
Peu	Not much / Little
Plus	More / No more
Presque	Almost
Tout	All
Très	Very

Adverbs of affirmation and negation

Oui	Yes
Non	No
Vraiment	Really
Volontiers	Gladly
Aussi	Too
Certainement	Certainly

Adverbs of doubt

Peut-être	Maybe
Probablement	Probably
Sans doute	Probable / Doubtless
Apparemment	Apparently
Vraisemblement	In all probability

Note: You can find more adverbs in each category.

La place des adverbes
Position of adverbs

Simple tenses

In simple tenses, the adverbs follow the verb.

e.g., Il parle rapidement → He speaks rapidely.
    Elle chante bien → She sings well.

> *Note: Simple tenses are tenses like the present, the perfect, the simple future, and the conditional...*

Compound tenses

Common adverbs

Common adverbs and some adverbs of manner are placed between the auxiliary verb and the past participle. Some of these are:

French	English
Assez	Enough
Bien	Well / Good
Beaucoup	A lot / Many
Bientôt	Soon
Déjà	Yet
Encore	Again / Still / yet
Enfin	Finally
Jamais	Never
Mal	Bad

Mieux	Better
Moins	Less
Souvent	Often
Toujours	Always
Trop	Too
Vite	Fast / Quickly

e.g., Elle a beaucoup parlé → She spoke a lot.

Elle est vite descendue → She came downstairs quickly.

Note: More adverbs follow this rule.

Adverbs of places

Adverbs of place and certain adverbs ending in "-ment" or certain adverbs of time as listed, usually follow the past participle.

Adverbs of time	*English*
Hier	Yesterday
Aujourd'hui	Today
Demain	Tomorrow
Avant-hier	The day before yesterday
Après-demain	The day after tomorrow
Tard	Late
Tôt	Early

e.g., Elle veut voyager partout → She wants to travel everywhere.

Elle est arrivée tard → She arrived late.

Adverbs changing position

<u>Adverbs modifying an infinitive verb</u>
The adverb that modifies an infinitive verb can be placed before or after it. It usually goes with modal verbs.

e.g., Je voudrais toujours voyager → I would always like to travel.
     Je voudrais voyager toujours → I would always like to travel.

Note : Modal verbs are "pouvoir," "vouloir," "devoir," and "savoir."

<u>Adverbs modifying a whole sentence</u>
Some adverbs may appear at the beginning or the end of a sentence when they modify the entire sentence.

e.g., Finalement, elle est arrivée → Finally, she arrived.
     Elle est arrivée finalement → She arrived finally.

<u>Adverbs of time</u>
Many adverbs of time may also appear at the beginning of a sentence even if the main rule is to place them after the conjugated verb.

e.g., Aujourd'hui, nous allons au cinéma → Today, we are going to the cinema.
     Demain, nous partirons → Tomorrow, we will leave.

vocabulaire de la cuisine
The vocabulary of the kitchen

Un placard	A cupboard
L'évier	The sink
Le robinet	The faucet / Tap
Le réfrigérateur / Le frigo	The fridge
Le congélateur / Le congel	The freezer
La gazinière	The gas stove
La hotte	The cooker hood
Le four	The oven
Le four à micro-ondes	The microwaves
Le mixer batter	The mixer
Le mixer broyeur	The blender
Le fouet	The whisk
Le hachoir	The mincer
Le grille-pain	The toaster
La bouilloire	The kettle
La passoire	The colander / The sieve
La friteuse	The deep fryer
La casserole	The saucepan
La poêle	The frying pan
Une sous-tasse	A saucer
Un saladier	A salad bowl
Un ouvre boîte	A can opener
Un tire-bouchon	A corkscrew

Un ouvre bouteille	A bottle opener
Un épluche légume	A vegetable peeler
Une planche à découper	A chopping board
Une spatule	A spatula
Une louche	A ladle
Un tablier	An apron

Note : "une sous-tasse" is also called "une soucoupe."

Note : "un épluche légume" is also called " un économe."

Le futur proche
The near future

When to use it?

The near future is used in French to express an action that will take place in the very near future (the next 24 hours). It is also used for future actions that are certain to happen.

e.g., Je vais aller au cinéma ce soir → I am going to go to the cinema.
Nous allons aller en France en Mai → We are going to go to France in May.

What does it mean in English?

This tense in English has the meaning of "going to" in a sentence like: "I am going to do something."

How to form it?

Subject + "aller" in the present tense + infinitive verb + ….

"Aller" in the present tense

Je vais
Tu vas
Il / Elle / On va
Nous allons
Vous allez
Ils / Elles vont

Note: Don't forget to use the "z" link for "nous" and "vous."

Examples

Je vais partir → I am going to leave.

Tu vas manger avec Paul ce soir → You are going to eat with Paul tonight.

Elle va dormir à l'hôtel → She is going to sleep at the hotel.

Note: As you can see, this tense is really easy to form, and there is no future tense involved. We are using the present tense of "aller" followed by an infinitive verb, and this gives us a future meaning.

Note: Even if we use the present tense of "aller," it is absolutely fine to use "aller" as an infinitive verb after it.
e.g., Je vais aller au restaurant → I am going to the restaurant.

Note: This tense is allowed in speaking even when the actions in the future are uncertain. I will advise you to use adverbs of doubt in this case.
e.g., Je vais peut-être aller en France en 2020 → I maybe going to France in 2020.

Note: It is also fine to have a double infinitive verb in your sentence as some vocabulary words include a verb like sports or activities (hobby).
e.g., On va aller regarder un film → We are going to watch a movie.
Je vais aller faire du ski cet hiver→ I am going to (do) ski this winter.

Le vocabulaire du linge de maison
The vocabulary of the household linen

Un drap plat	A flat sheet
Un drap housse	A fitted sheet
Une parure de lit	A bed linen set
Une taie d'oreiller	A pillowcase
Une housse de couette	A duvet cover
Une nappe	A tablecloth
Une serviette	A serviette
Un set de table	A table set
Un chemin de table	A table runner
Une serviette de bain	A towel
Un torchon	A tea towel
Un peignoir	A bathrobe
Un tapis de table	A table mat

L'expression de la durée
The expression of time and duration

How does it work?

There are different ways in French to express time and duration. Using some prepositions, adverbs, locutions, and others is possible.

Prepostions

Different prepositions can express time and duration.

"En"

The preposition "en" introduces the time needed to complete something.

e.g., Je peux courir 10km en 40 minutes → I can run 10k in 40 minutes.

> *Note: The verb in the sentence can be conjugated in the present, the past, or the future tense.*

"Dans"

The preposition "dans" is used to introduce something that is going to happen.

e.g., Je vais en France dans 2 semaines → I am going to France in two weeks.

> *Note: The verb in the sentence can be conjugated in the present or the future tense.*

"Depuis"

The preposition "depuis" introduces the beginning of an action in the past when the action is still going on in the present.

e.g., J'habite en France depuis 2 ans → I have been living in France for two years.

> *Note: The verb in the sentence can only be conjugated in the present tense even if the action started in the past because the action is still going on.*

"Pendant"

The preposition "pendant" introduces the duration of a past, a future, or habitual action.

e.g., J'ai fais du ski pendant les vacances → I did skiing during the holiday.

> *Note: The verb in the sentence can be conjugated in the present (habitual actions), the past (completed actions), or the future tense (limited action in the time).*

> *Note: Sometimes we can omit "pendant" especially in sentences using the perfect tense.*
> *e.g., J'ai habité un an en France → J'ai habité pendant un an en France.*

"Pour"

The preposition "pour" introduces the time in which we are doing something.

e.g., Je vais partir pour six mois → I am going to leave for six months.

Note: The verb in the sentence can be conjugated in the present, the past, or the future tense.

Adverbs

The adverb "jusqu'à" introduces the moment when the action stops.

e.g., Je suis resté jusqu'à minuit → I stayed until midnight.

Note: The verb in the sentence can be conjugated in the present, the past, or the future tense.

Note: Don't forget to use it after movement verbs. Without the meaning will be "in" and not "to."
e.g., Je marche jusqu'au parc → I am walking to the park.
Je marche au parc → I am walking in the park.

Locutions

"Il y a"

The locution "il y a" introduces the time passed between a past action and the moment we speak.

e.g., Je suis allé en France il y a 6 mois → I went to France six months ago.

Note: The verb in the sentence can only be conjugated in the past tense.

"À partir de"

The locution "à partir de" introduces the moment when the action starts.

e.g., À partir de lundi, j'apprends le français → I am learning French from Monday.

> *Note: The verb in the sentence can be conjugated in the present or future tense.*

"Au bout de"

The locution "au bout de" introduces the moment at the end of which the action happens.

e.g., La machine à laver s'arrête au bout de deux heures → The washing machine stops after two hours.

> *Note: The verb in the sentence can be conjugated in the present (for habitual actions), the past, or the future tense.*

Constructions

"Il y a … que"

The construction "il y a … que" is used as an equivalent of "depuis."

e.g., Il y a 3 ans que j'habite en France → I have been living in France for three years.

J'habite en France depuis 3 ans → I have been living in France for three years.

"Ça fait … que"

The construction "ça fait … que" is used as an equivalent of "depuis".

e.g., Ça fait 3 ans que j'habite en France → I have been living in France for three years.

"De … à …"

The construction "de… à" introduces limits in time.

e.g., J'ai un rendez-vous de 10 heures à midi → I have an appointment from 10 am till 12 pm.

> *Note: The verb in the sentence can be conjugated in the present (for habitual actions), the past, or the future tense.*

"Depuis que …"

The construction "depuis … que" is used as the beginning of an action that started in the past.

e.g., Depuis que je parle bien français je vais souvent en France → Since I speak French well, I often go to France.

Le futur simple
The simple future

When to use it ?

The future simple is a tense used to refer to an uncertain future action like plans or forecasts.

What does it mean in English?

The future simple will be translated by "will" plus a verb.

e.g., J'irai en France l'été prochain → I will go to France next summer.

How to form it?

Subject + infinitive verb + future endings + ...

> *Note: As you can see, the simple future tense requires the infinitive form of the verb. The reason is that we need an "r" sound before their endings to form this tense so when we hear it, we know it talks about the future.*

The endings

All the verbs (-er, -ir, irregular verbs) in the future simple have the same endings.

Je	-ai
Tu	-as
Il / Elle / On	-a
Nous	-ons
Vous	-ez
Ils / Elles	-ont

How to turn "-er" verbs into simple future

To turn "-er" verbs into simple future simply use the endings above at the end of the infinitive verb.

e.g., Manger → Je mangerai.
     Parler → Il parlera.

Note: The verb "aller" being irregular, doesn't follow this rule.

Note: In the simple future, the verbs ending in –yer, turn their "y" into an "i" for "je, tu, il, elle, on, ils, and elles."
e.g., S'ennuyer → Je m'ennuierai.
     Essayer → Tu essaieras.

Note: For these verbs, the pronunciation between the infinitive verb and its future tense will change. The "e" before the "r" is silent.
e.g., S'ennuyer → Je m'ennuierai.
     Essayer → Tu essaieras.

How to turn "-ir" verbs into simple future

To turn "-ir" verbs (regular and irregular ones) into simple future simply use the endings above at the end of the infinitive verb.

e.g., Partir → Je partirai.
     Finir → Nous finirons.

How to turn "-re" verbs in to simple future

All "-re" verbs are irregular verbs. To turn them into simple future, simply drop off the "e" at the end of the infinitive verb and add the endings above after the "r."

e.g., Dire → Je dirai.
     Lire → Elle lira.

> Note: "Faire" and "être" being irregular verbs, don't follow this rule.

How to turn irregular verbs into simple future

The other irregular verbs are really irregular, so you need to learn them by heart.

Irregular verbs	Simple future for "je"
Devoir	Je devrai
Falloir	Il faudra
Savoir	Je saurai
Venir	Je viendrai
Devenir	Je deviendrai
Revenir	Je reviendrai
Voir	Je verrai
Pouvoir	Je pourrai
Vouloir	Je voudrai
Être	Je serai
Avoir	J'aurai
Faire	Je ferai
Aller	J'irai

Note: Remember "falloir" can only be used with the subject "il."

Note: To find these irregular verbs for the other subjects simply replace "je" and "ai" for the subject you need and its future ending.

Note: There are other irregular verbs apart from the ones listed above.

Le vocabulaire de la propriété
The vocabulary of property

Une maison	A house
Un appartement	An apartment
Un studio	A studio
Une villa	A villa
Une maison de campagne	A country house
Une maison secondaire	A holiday home
Une boîte aux lettres	Letterbox
Un voisin	A neighbour
Un locataire	A tenant
Un propriétaire	A landlord/Landlady
Une sonnette	A doorbell
Une serrure	A door lock
Un portail	A vehicle gate/An entrance
Un verrou	A lock
Un jardin	A garden
Un potager	A vegetable garden
Un clôture	A fence/A wire fence
Un abri de jardin	A shed
Une cave	A cellar
Un barrière	A barrier
Une véranda	A conservatory
Une piscine	A swimming pool

Le comparatif
The comparative

What is it?

The comparative is used to express the degree of superiority or inferiority in quality, quantity or intensity.

How to form it?

French comparative can be formed with an adjective, an adverb, a noun, or a verb.

The comparative of adjectives agree in gender and number with the subject of the sentence.

Comparative of adjectives and adverbs

Formation

The comparative is formed by placing "plus," "moins" or "aussi" before the adjective or the adverb and "que" after it.

Degree	Comparative	English
Superiority	Plus ... que	More ... than
Egality	Aussi ... que	As ... as
Inferiority	Moins ... que	Less ... than

e.g., Cette robe est plus belle que l'autre → This dress is prettier than the other.
Elles sont aussi intelligentes que moi → They are as intelligent as I am.
Je parle moins vite que Paul → I speak less quicly than Paul.

With a disjunctive pronoun

If you want to use a disjunctive pronoun in the comparative, it will follow "que."

e.g., Je suis plus intelligente que lui → I am more intelligent than him.

<u>In negative sentences</u>

In negative sentences "aussi", "plus," and "moins" stay.

e.g., Elle ne parle pas aussi vite que lui→ She doesn't speak as fast as him.

> *Note: In negative sentences "aussi" can become "si." but in speaking it is rarely used with "que."*
> *e.g., Elle ne parle pas si vite (que son frère).*

Comparative of nouns

<u>Formation</u>
Followed by a noun, the comparative forms change.

Degree	Comparative	English
Superiority	Plus de … que	More … than
Egality	Autant de … que	As many/much … as
Inferiority	Moins de … que	Less … than

e.g., J'ai plus de livres que Paul → I have more books than Paul.
     J'ai autant de livres que Paul → I have as many books as Paul.
     J'ai moins de livres que Paul → I have less books than Paul.

<u>With a disjunctive pronoun</u>
If you want to use a disjunctive pronoun in the comparative, it will follow "que."

e.g., J'ai plus de livres que lui → I have more textbooks than him.

<u>In negative sentences</u>
In negative sentences "plus de", "autant de," and "moins de" stay.

e.g., Je n'ai pas plus de livres que Paul → I don't have more textbook than Paul.
     Je n'ai jamais autant de chance que lui → I never have as much luck as him.

Comparative of verbs

Formation
Preceded by a verb, the comparative forms change.

Degree	Comparative	English
Superiority	Plus … que	More … than
Egality	Autant … que	As … as
Inferiority	Moins … que	Less … than

e.g., Je dors plus que Paul → I sleep more than Paul.
     Je mange autant que Paul → I eat as much as Paul.
     Je parle moins que Paul → I speak less than Paul.

With a disjunctive pronoun
If you want to use a disjunctive pronoun in the comparative, it will follow "que."

e.g., Je dors plus que lui → I sleep more than him.

In negative sentences
In negative sentences "plus que", "autant que," and "moins que" stay.

e.g., Je ne parle pas moins que Paul → I don't speak less than Paul.
     Je ne travaille plus moins que toi → I am no longer working less than you.

Le superlatif
The superlative

What is it?

The superlative is used to express the highest or the lowest degree of quality.

e.g., Le plus gentil → The nicest. (masculine)
    Les moins gentil → The least nice. (masculine / plural)

How do we form it?

The French superlative can be formed with an adjective, an adverb, a noun, or a verb. The superlative of an adjective agrees in gender and number with the subject of the sentence.

Superlative of adjectives

The superlative of an adjective is formed by adding "le," "la," or "les" to the comparative forms. The superlative will precede the adjective.

Comparative	Superlative	English
Plus … que	Le / la / les plus (de)	The most (-est)
Moins … que	Le / la / les moins (de)	The least

e.g., Pierre est le plus gentil garçon → Pierre is the nicest boy.
    Marie est la fille la plus intelligente → Marie is the most intelligent.

Note: "de" follows the superlative. "De" can mean "of" or "in."
e.g., Cette peinture est la plus belle de toutes → This painting is the most beautiful of all.
Pierre est le plus gentil garçon de la classe → Pierre is the nicest boy in the class.

Note: When a verb follows the superlative, it's usually in the subjunctive mood.
e.g., C'est le film le plus intéressant que j'aie vu → It's the most interesting movie I have seen.

Superlative of adverbs

The superlative of an adverb is formed by adding "le" to the comparative form. The superlative will precede the adverb.

Comparative	*Superlative*	*English*
Plus … que	Le plus	The most (-est)
Moins … que	Le moins	The least

e.g., Cette fille chante le plus fort → This girl sings the loudest.
Il court le moins vite → He runs the least fast.

Superlative of nouns

The superlative of a noun is formed by adding "le" to the comparative form. The superlative will precede the noun.

Comparative	*Superlative*	*English*
Plus de	Le plus de	The most (-est)
Moins de	Le moins de	The least

e.g., Il a le plus de livres → He has the most textbooks.

    Elle a le moins de chance → She has the least (of)luck.

The superlative of verbs

The superlative of a verb is formed by adding "le" to the comparative form. "que" isn't used. The superlative will follow the verb.

Comparative	Superlative	English
Plus que	Le plus	The most (-est)
Moins que	Le moins	The least

e.g., Tu dors le plus → You sleep the most.

    Elle boit le moins d'alcool → She drinks the least alcohol.

Negative sentences

The negation of the superlative follows the normal rules.

e.g., Paul n'est pas le plus grand → Paul is not the tallest.

    Marie n'est plus la plus rapide → Marie is no longer the fastest.

    Pierre ne mange pas le moins → Pierre doesn't eat the least.

    Paul n'a pas le plus de livres→ Paul doesn't have the most textbooks.

Le vocabulaire des vêtements
The vocabulary of clothes

Une robe	A dress
Une jupe	A skirt
Un gilet	A cardigan
Un jean	A pair of jeans
Un pull	A jumper
Un haut	A top
Un t-shirt	A t-shirt
Un pantalon	A pair of trousers
Un short	A pair of shorts
Un blazer	A blazer
Un soutien-gorge	A bra
Une culotte	Knickers
Un pyjama	A pyjamas
Des collants	Tights
Des chausettes	Socks
Un maillot de bain	A swimsuit
Une chemise	A shirt
Un costume	A suit
Une cravate	A tie
Une veste	A jacket
Un débardeur	A vest
Un calçon	A boxer

Les comparatifs et les superlatifs irréguliers
Irregular comparatives and superlatives

"Bon" and "bien"

The adjective "bon" means "good," and the adverb "bien" means "well." They are irregular in comparisons of superiority.

Adjective	Comparative	English	Superlative	English
Bon(s)	Meilleur(e)(s)	Better	Le / la / Les	The best
Bonne(s)			meilleur(e)(s)	

Adverb	Comparative	Englsih	Superlative	English
Bien	Mieux	Better	Le mieux	The best

e.g., Ce livre est meilleur que l'autre → This textbook is better than the other.

Ces pommes sont les meilleures → These apples are the best ones.

Elle parle mieux que lui → She speaks better than him.

Elle chante le mieux de toutes → She sings the best of all.

> Note: "Moins" and "aussi" are used with "bon" and "bien."
> e.g., Il chante aussi bien que toi → He sings as well as you.
>   Ce thé est moins bon que l'autre → This tea is less good than the other.

"Petit"

"Petit" is an adjective, and it means "small." It has regular and irregular forms. The irregular form is less common than the régular and mainly used when speaking or with an abstract sense.

	Comparative	English	Superlative	English
Regular form	Plus petit(e)(s)	Smaller	Le / la / les plus petit(e)(s)	The smallest
Irregular form	Moindre(s)	Lower	Le / la / les moindre(s)	The least

e.g., Ma voiture est plus petite que la sienne → My car is smaller than his (hers).

Cette boite est la plus petite → This box is the smallest.

Je n'ai pas la moindre idée → I don't have the least (slightest) idea.

Je suis parti en vacances à moindre coût → I went on holiday at a lower cost.

"Peu"

"peu" is an adverb and it means "little."

	Comparative	English	Superlative	English
Peu	Moins	Less	Le moins	The less

e.g., Marie parle le moins → Marie talks the less.

Pierre travaille moins que Paul → Pierre works less than Paul.

"Mauvais" and "mal"

The adjective "mauvais" means "bad," and the adverb "mal" means" badly."
They both have regular as well as irregular forms. The regular form of "mauvais"
is used in a concrete sense. Its irregular form is used in a moral sense. The
irregular form of "mal" is not commonly used.

Mauvais

	Comparative	English	Superlative	English
Regular form	Plus mauvais(e)(s)	Worse	Le / la / les plus mauvais(e)(s)	The worst
Irregular form	Pire	Worse	Le / la / les pire(s)	The worst

e.g., Ce livre est le plus mauvais de tous→ This textbook is the worst of all.
  Cette situation est la pire de toutes → This Situation is the worst of all.
  Ce livre est plus mauvais que l'autre → This book is worse than the other.
  Cette situation est pire que l'autre → This situation is worse than the other.

Mal

	Comparative	English	Superlative	English
Regular form	Plus mal	Worse	Le plus mal	The worst
Irregular form	Pis	Worse	Le pis	The worst

e.g., Il chante plus mal que Marie → He sings worse than Marie.
  Il chante pis que Marie → He sings worse than Marie.
  Il chante le plus mal de tous → He sings the worst of all.
  Il chante le pis de tous → He sings the worst of all.

"Beaucoup"

The adverb "Beaucoup" means "a lot." It has two comparative form, "plus" and "davantage" which means "more."

	Comparative	English	Superlative	English
Beaucoup	Plus	More	Le plus	The most

e.g., Marie à plus de livres → Marie has more textbooks.

Marie à le plus de livres → Marie has the most textbooks.

Note: "davantage" is used to indicate a comparison of superiority and is generally placed at the end of the sentence.

e.g., Elle est intelligente, sa fille l'est davantage → She is intelligent; her daughter is even more.

Le vocabulaire des accessoires
The vocabulary of the accessories

Des chaussures	Shoes
Des baskets	Trainers
Des compensées	Wedges
Des talons	Heels
Des talons aiguilles	Stiletto
Des ballerines	Flat pumps
Des sandales	Sandals
Des tongs	Flip flops
Des bijoux	Jewels
Un colier	A necklace
Un bracelet	A bracelet
Des boucles d'oreilles	Earrings
Une bague	A ring
Une montre	A watch
Un sac à main	A handbag
Un portefeuille	A wallet
Un porte-monnaie	A purse
Une pochette	A clutch
Une bandoulière	A shoulder strap
Une ceinture	A belt
Un foulard	A light scarf
Une écharpe	A scarf

Un béret	A beret
Un chapeau	A hat
Un bonnet	A winter hat / A beanie hat
Une casquette	A cap
Des lunettes	Glasses
Des lunettes de soleil	Sunglasses

L'infinitif
The infinitive form

What is it?

The infinitive is the unconjugated form of a verb.

e.g., Manger → To eat.

When is it used?

<u>After some prepositions</u>
The infinitive is used after the prepositions "de," "à," "pour," and "sans." In the English translation, the present participle is sometimes used instead of the infinitive.

e.g., Je vais voir Marie avant de partir → I am going to see Marie before leaving.
Je prends le train pour aller à Paris → I am taking the train to go to Paris.
Je vais faire à manger → I am going to cook.
Il traverse sans regarder → He is crossing without looking.

<u>After a modal verb</u>
The infinitive is used after a conjugated modal verb. The French modal verbs are "pouvoir," "devoir," "vouloir," and "savoir."

e.g., Je dois aller à Paris pour le travail → I have to go to Paris for work.

Note: Every time there are two verbs: one after the other, the first one needs to be conjugated, and the second one needs to be in the infinitive form.
e.g., Je l'ai vu danser hier → I saw him dancing yesterday.

<u>After "Après"</u>
After "après" the infinitive of "avoir" or "être" plus the past participle are used.

e.g., Après avoir parlé → After having spoken.
    Après être parti → After having left.

<u>As an imperative</u>
This infinitive verb can be used as an imperative to express a command or advice.

e.g., Ne pas fumer → Do not smoke.
    Laisser cuire pendant 30 minutes → Allow to cook for thirty minutes.

> *Note: it is common to see the infinitive used as an imperative in recipes, manuals, and instructions.*

In negative sentences

In negative sentences, the whole negation goes before the infinitive verb.

e.g., Je vais en France pour ne pas avoir de pluie → I am going to France to have no rain.

> *Note: "ne pas," "ne plus," "ne jamais," "ne que," and "ne rien" can be used.*

Les expressions avec "être" et "avoir"
Expressions with "to be" and "to have"

Expressions with "être"

As in English, most of the following expressions are using "to be."

French	*English*
Être en train de	To be in the process of
Être à	To belong to
Être de	To be from
Être égal	To make no difference
Être de retour	To be back
Ça y est	It's done
Être en avance	To be early
Être en retard	To be late

Note: "être en train de" must be followed by an infinitive verb.
e.g., Je suis en train de regarder un film → I am watching a movie.

Note: "être à" can be followed by a proper noun, an article, and a noun or a possessive adjective and a noun.
e.g., La voiture est à Marie → The car belongs to Marie.

Expressions with "avoir"

Unlike in English, all the following expressions are using "to have" instead of "to be."

66

French	English
French	*English*
Avoir chaud	To be hot / To be warm
Avoir froid	To be cold
Avoir faim	To be hungry
Avoir soif	To be thirsty
Avoir sommeil	To be tired / To be sleepy
Avoir peur (de)	To be scared (of)
Avoir honte (de)	To be ashamed (of)
Avoir raison	To be right
Avoir tort	To be wrong
Avoir mal à	To have an ache in
Avoir lieu	To take place
Avoir beau	To do something in vain
Avoir l'air (de)	To seem to
Avoir de la chance	To be lucky
Avoir du retard	To be late
Avoir (hours/minutes) de retard	To be late by
Avoir (hours/minutes) d'avance	To be early by
Avoir envie de	To want
Avoir besoin de	To have a need of
Avoir l'habitude de	To be used to
Avoir l'occasion de	To have the chance to
Avoir l'intention de	To intend to
Avoir le temps de	To have the time to
Avoir (number) ans	To have (number) years old

Note: The expressions with "de" can be followed by a proper noun, a disjunctive pronoun, an article, and a noun, a possessive adjective and a noun or an infinitive verb.

e.g., J'ai peur des serpents → I am scared of snakes.

J'ai peur de conduire → I am scared of driving.

Note: "avoir mal à" can be followed by an article and a noun.

e.g., J'ai mal à la tête → I have a headache.

Les pronoms possessifs
The possessive pronouns

What is it?

A possessive pronoun is used in place of a noun to refer to possessions and belongings.

The possessives pronouns

Masculine Singular	Feminine Singular	Masculine plural	Feminine plural	English
Le mien	La mienne	Les miens	Les miennes	Mine
Le tien	La tienne	Les tiens	Les tiennes	Yours
Le sien	La sienne	Les siens	Les siennes	His/Hers/Its
Le nôtre	La nôtre	Les nôtres	Les nôtres	Ours
Le vôtre	La vôtre	Les vôtres	Les vôtres	Yours
Le leur	La leur	Les leurs	Les leurs	Theirs

When are they used?

The possessive pronouns are used to replace a possessive adjective plus a noun to avoid repetitions.

e.g., J'aime ma voiture et pas la vôtre → I like my car and not yours.

Ce sont mes livres et pas les tiens → They are my textbooks and not yours.

Ma robe est rouge, la tienne est jaune → My dress is red; yours is yellow.

How to use them?

<u>The main rule</u>
The possessive pronouns must agree with the noun they replace, as a result, they must be accompanied by the appropriate definite article or one of its contracted form "au," "à la," "à l'," "aux," "du," "de la," "de l'," or "des"

e.g., Je vais à mon cours de français et toi au tien → I am going to my French class and you to yours.

<u>With some indefinite pronoun subjects</u>
The pronouns "le sien," "la sienne," "les siens," and "les siennes" will be used when the possessor is an indefinite pronoun subject such as, "on," "personne," "tout le monde," or "chacun."

e.g., On aime sa famille → On aime la sienne.

<u>With "chacun"</u>
The possessive pronoun will agree with the subject of the sentence when a plural subject is modified by "chacun."

e.g., Nous avons chacun les nôtres → We each have ours.

<u>Special meaning</u>
In the masculine plural, the possessive pronouns designate relatives, friends, or allies.

e.g., Il est des nôtres → He is one of us.

Le vocabulaire de la trousse de toilette
The vocabulary of the toilet bag

Une crème	A cream
Un dentifrice	Toothpaste
Un déodorant	A deodorant
Du gel	Gel
De la laque	Hairspray
Du maquillage	Makeup
Une brosse à cheveux	A hairbrush
Une brosse à dents	A toothbrush
Une barrette	A hair clip
Un élastique	A hair band
Une pince	A hair grip
Du démaquillant	Makeup remover
Du cotton	Cotton pad
Un cotton tige	A cotton bud
Du parfum	Perfume
Du savon	Soap
Du gel douche	Shower gel
Du shampooing	Shampoo
De l'après-shampooing	Conditioner
Un couple ongles	A nail clipper
Une lime à ongle	A nail file
Une pince à épiler	A tweezer

Un rasoir	A razor
Un vernis à ongles	A nail varnish
Du dissolvant	Nail varnish remover

Les pronoms démonstratifs
The demonstrative pronouns

What is it?

A demonstrative pronoun is used to point something specific within a sentence.

When to use them?

Demonstrative pronouns are used to indicate items in space or time.

The indefinite pronouns

They can be singular or plural.

French	English
Celui (m)	That / This / The one
Celle (f)	That / This / The one
Ceux (m/p)	Those / These / The one
Celles (f/p)	Those / These / The one

How to use them?

The simple form
They are used to replace a whole sentence, or a part of a sentence with a noun to avoid repetitions. The simple form is used when the object of the sentence is followed by "de."

e.g., J'aime la robe de Marie! → I like Marie's dress.
    Moi je préfére celle de Laura! → Me, I prefer Laura's (own).

Note: The demonstrative pronouns can also be followed by a relative pronoun such as "que."

e.g., C'est l'enfant que tu gardes? → Oui, c'est celui que je garde.

Is it the child you are looking after? → Yes, it is the one I am looking after.

The compound forms

The compound form of the demonstrative pronouns is formed by adding "-ci" or "-là" after the pronouns. "-ci" will be used for something near in the distance and "-là" for something far in the distance.

French	*English*
Celui-ci / Celui-là	This one / That one
Celle-ci / Celle-là	This one / That one
Ceux-ci / Ceux-là	These ones / Those ones
Celles-ci / Celles-là	These ones / Those ones

e.g., Tu veux celui-ci ou celui-là? → Do you want this one or that one?

J'aime la robe rouge mais je préfére celle-là → I like the red dress, but I prefer that one.

Note: In the spoken language, the compound form is used with a gesture, so we often point to the object in the sentence while speaking.

Les expressions avec "faire" et "aller"

Expressions with "to do" and "to go"

Expressions with "faire"

Unlike in English, all the following expressions use "to have" instead of "to do."

French	English
Il fait nuit	It is dark (weather)
Il fait jour	It is light (weather)
Faire l'impossible	To do the impossible
Faire de son mieux	To do one's best
Faire du bien (à)	To do some good
Faire fortune	To make a fortune
Faire des économies	To save money
Faire plaisir (à)	To please
Faire mal (à)	To hurt
Se faire mal (à)	To hurt oneself
Faire attention (à)	To pay attention (to)
Faire peur (à)	To scare
Faire confiance (à)	To trust
Faire la connaissance de	To meet someone
Faire les courses	To do the grocery shopping
Faire la cuisine	To cook
Faire à manger (à)	To do the cooking
Faire les devoirs	To do the homework

Faire un jogging	To jog
Faire la queue (à)	To queue
Faire exprès	To do something on purpose
Faire semblant	To pretend
Ça ne fait rien	It doesn't matter

Note: The expressions with "à" can be followed by a proper noun, an article, and a noun or by a possessive adjective and a noun. "Se faire mal à" can only be followed by an article and a noun as it is a reflexive verb.
e.g., Je fais la queue au magasin → I am queuing at the shop.
Il a fait mal à Paul → He hurt Paul.
Je me suis fait mal à la jambe → I hurt my leg.

Note: "faire la connaissance de" can be followed by a proper noun, an article, and a noun or by a possessive adjective and a noun.
e.g., J'ai fais la connaissance de ton voisin → I have met your neighbour.
J'ai fait la connaissance de Paul → I have met Paul.

Expressions with "aller"

As in English, some of the following expressions are using "to go."

French	*English*
Aller à la pêche	To go fishing
Aller à la chasse	To go hunting
Aller à pied	To go by foot / To walk
Aller loin	To go far
Aller trop loin	To go too far
Aller bien	To feel well

Aller mal	To feel bad
Aller mieux	To feel better
Aller à	To suit
Aller bien à	To suit well

Note: "aller à" can be followed by a proper noun, an article, and a noun or by a possessive adjective and a noun. "Se faire mal à" can only be followed by an article and a noun as it is a reflexive verb.

e.g., Cette veste irait à Paul → This jacket would suit Paul.

Les pronoms indéfinis
The indefinite pronouns

What is it?

An indefinite pronoun is a pronoun that does not refer to any person, amount, or thing in particular.

e.g., anything, something …

The indefinite pronouns

French	*English*
Aucun(e)	Not any / none / Not one
Autre(s)	Other(s)
L'autre	The other / The other one
Les autres	The others / The other ones
L'un(e) …. L'autre	The one … the other
Les uns (unes) … les autres	The ones …. The others
L'un ou l'autre	Either one
L'un et l'autre	Both
Ni l'un(e) ni l'autre	Neither one
L'un(e) à l'autre	To each other
L'un(e) pour l'autre	One for the other
Autre chose	Anything else / Something else
Certain(e)(s)	Certain /Some
Chacun(e)(s)	Each one / Everyone
Pas grand-chose	Not much

Le (la) même (chose)	The same
Les mêmes (choses)	The same
On	One / They / People
Personne ne	No one / Nobody
Plusieurs	Several
Quelqu'un	Someone
Quelqu'un d'autre	Someone else
Quelques-un(e)(s) de	Some of
Quelque chose	Something
Quelque chose d'autre	Something else
Rien	Nothing
Tout(e)(s)	All / Everything
Tout le monde	Everyone / Everybody

Note: There are other indefinite pronouns than these listed above.

Le vocabulaire des étapes de la vie
The vocabulary of life stages

Birth

La naissance	The birth
La vie	The life
Un bébé	A baby
Un enfant	A child
Un nouveau-né	A new born
Des jumeaux / Des jumelles	Twins
La grossesse	The pregnancy
Accoucher	To give birth
Allaiter	To breastfeed
Donner le biberon	To bottle feed
Attendre un enfant	To expect a baby
Avoir des enfants	To have children
Marcher à quatre pattes	To crawl
Le baptème	The christening

Childhood and youth

L'enfance	The childhood
La jeunesse	The youth
Un jeune	A youth
Un jeune homme	A young man
Une jeune fille	A young woman

Un adolescent	A teenager
Bien élévé(e)	Well mannered
Mal élévé(e)	Bad mannered
Elever un enfant	To bring up a child
Être majeur	To be of age
Être diplômé(e)	To graduate
Faire un stage	To do an internship
Étudier	To study
Entrer à l'école	To start school

Adulthood

L'age adulte	Adulthood
Un adulte	An adult
Une grande personne	A grown up
Se marier	To get married
Le marié / La mariée	The groom / The bride
Un mariage	A wedding
Un enterrement de vie de garçon	A stag do
Un enterrement de vie de jeune fille	A hen party
Une cérémonie	A ceremony
Un événement	An event
S'installer	To settle down
Emménager	To move in
Une pendaison de crémaillère	A housewarming
Chercher un travail	To look for a job
Avoir une promotion	To be promoted

Une étape	A stage
Être mature	To be mature/grown up
Être responsable	To be responsible

> *Note: More vocabulary can be found in the beginners' book volume 1.*

Old age

La vieillesse	The old age
Une personne agée	An old person
La maison de retraite	Old people's home
Sage	Wise
Un enterrement	Burial
Les funerailles	Funeral
Un testament	A will
Prendre sa retarite	To retire
Être à la retraite	To retire
Un(e) retraité(e)	A retired person / A retiree
Être gaga	To dote
Mourir	To die
La mort	The death / The dead
Enterrer	To bury
Heriter	To inherit

Les pronoms démonstratifs indéfinis
The indefinite demonstrative pronouns

What are they?

They are invariable demonstrative pronouns used in the singular form only. They have no plural, and they are followed by the singular form of the verb for the subject "il."

Le pronom "ce"

"Ce" means "it." It becomes "c'" in front of a vowel or "h." It usually precedes a conjugated form of the verb "être" except in questions, where it will follow it. "C'est" will then become "est-ce." "Ce sont" is used when the subject is in the plural. "Ce" is used in front of different things, as listed below.

<u>With être</u>
"Ce" is used when the conjugated form of "être" starts with a consonant, but it becomes "c'" when it starts with a vowel.

e.g., C'est beau → It is beautiful.
     Ce serait très bien → It would be really/very nice.

> *Note: "ce" in front of the verb "être" is used for more things as described in the lesson on the differences between "il est" and "c'est." You'll find this lesson in the beginners' book volume 1.*

<u>Before a preposition</u>
"ce" and "c'" are used in front of a preposition introducing an infinitive verb or not. "Ce" will be used in front of a consonant and "c'" in front of a vowel.

e.g., C'est pour toi → It is for you.

Before a relative pronoun
"Ce" is used in front of a relative pronoun when the idea behind the relative pronoun is not given.

e.g., Elle a toujours ce qu'elle veut → She always has what she wants.
    Elle a toujours les choses qu'elle veut → She always has the things she wants.

Before a superlative
"Ce" and "c'" are used in front of a superlative. "Ce" will be used in front of a consonant and "c'" in front of a vowel.

e.g., Ce sont les meilleures cerises → These are the best cherries.
    C'est le meilleur restaurant de Nice → It is the best restaurant in Nice.

> *Note: "ce" is also used to designate or show something or someone.*

> *Note: "ce" is also used in front of "devoir" and "pouvoir."*
> *e.g., Ce doit être elle → It must be her.*
> *   Ce peut être elle → It may be her.*

Les pronoms "ceci" and "cela"

"Ceci" means "this" and "cela" means "that." "Ceci" is used when referring to what is going to be said and "cela" is used to refer to what has been said. They can be used with every verb, including "être."

e.g., Rapellez-vous de ceci, la grammaire est facile → Remember this, grammar is easy.

La grammaire est facile, rappellez-vous de cela → Grammar is easy, remember that.

Note: "ceci" and "cela" are used more commonly in writing than speaking. In the spoken language, we prefer to use "ça" instead of "ceci" or "cela." "Ça" means "it," "this," or "that."
e.g., La grammaire est facile, rappellez-vous de ça → Grammar is easy, remember that.

Note: "ça" is also used in front of "devoir" and "pouvoir."
e.g., Ça doit être elle → It must be her.
*   Ça peut être elle → It may be her.*

Note: when the conjugated form of "être" doesn't start with a vowel, it is possible to use "ce" or "ça."
e.g., Ce serait bien / ça serait bien → It would be great.
*   Ce sera bien / ça sera bien → It will be great.*

Differences between "ce" and "ça"

"Ça" is invariable and it replaces "ceci" and "cela" and is used with other verbs than "être." "Ça" can also be used with "être" sometimes. "Ce" is only used with "être." Its plural form is "ce sont."

e.g., C'est lui qui chante bien → It is him who is singing well.
   Ça ne fait rien ! → It doesn't matter.

Note: with "être." "cela" can sometimes be replaced by "ce" rather than "ça."

e.g., Cela n'est pas grave → That is not important.

    Ce n'est pas très grave → It is not really / very important.

    Ça n'est pas grave → It is not important.

Le vocabulaire de la vie familliale
Vocabulary of family life

Le mariage	The wedding
La lune de miel	The honeymoon
Les noces d'or	Golden wedding anniversary
L'anniversaire	Birthday
L'anniversaire de mariage	Wedding anniversary
La rencontre	The meeting
Un amant	A lover
Une maîtresse	A misstress
Le foyer familial	Parental home
Un rendez-vous	A date / An appointment
Un rencard	A date
Un bisous	A kiss
S'embrasser	To kiss each other
L'amour	The love
La tendresse	The tenderness
La passion	The passion
Être fidèle	To be faithful
Être infidèle	To be unfaithful
Tromper	To cheat on someone
Commettre un adultère	To commit adultery
Se réconcillier	To reconcile with each other
Être ensemble	To be together

Les pronoms relatifs
The relative pronouns

What is it?

A relative pronoun represents and replaces the noun placed before it. A relative pronoun introduces a clause which is a complement to the noun. This clause is then called a relative subordinate clause.

The relative pronouns

Qui

"Qui" functions as the subject of a clause and can refer to either a person or a thing. It means "who." "which," or "that." A conjugated verb always follows "qui".

e.g., La femme qui parle est ma mère → The woman who speaks/is speaking is my mother.

Le livre qui est sur la table est bien → The textbook which is on the table is good.

> *Note: "Qui" is also used in some archaic idiomatic expressions to replace "ce qui," for example, "qui plus est,".*

Que

"Que" functions as the direct object of a clause and can refer to either persons or things. It becomes "qu'" before a vowel. "Que" means "whom." "which," or "that." A subject follows it.

e.g., Le garçon que nous avons vu → The boy that we saw.

Les livres qu'elle écrit → The textbooks that she is writing.

Ce qui

"Ce qui" is used as the subject of a clause when there is no antecedent. It means "what," "that," or "which." A verb follows it.

e.g., Comprenez-vous ce qui se passe? → Do you understand what is happening?
   Ce qui est arrivé est impossible → What happened is impossible.

> Note: "ce qui" can be combined with "tout."
> e.g., Tout ce qui est bon est beau → All that is good is beautiful.

Ce que

"Ce que" is used as the object of a verb in a relative clause when there is no antecedent. It has the same meaning of "que" and a subject follows it.

e.g., Je comprends ce que vous dites → I understand what you are saying.
   Ce qu'il dit est difficile à comprendre → What he says is difficult to understand.

> Note: "ce que" can be combined with "tout."
> e.g., Tout ce qu'elle fait est bon → All that she does is good.

À qui

"À qui" used as the object of clause refers to people only. It means "to whom."

e.g., La fille à qui vous parler est gentille → The girl to whom you are speaking is nice.

Note: "qui" can be preceded by other prepositions depending on the meaning you want.
e.g., Pour qui → For whom.
De qui → Of whom.

Lequel, laquelle, lesquels, lesquelles

The forms of "lequel" are used after a preposition, and they refer to things or people and must agree with the antecedent. They mean "which."

e.g., La maison dans laquelle ... → The house in which...

Le restaurant devant lequel... → The restaurant in front of which...

Les raisons pour lesquelles... → The reasons why...

Note: After "parmi" (among) et "entre" (between) the forms of "lequel" are obligatory when referring to people. "Qui" cannot be used.
e.g., Les gens parmi lesquels il vit → The people among whom he lives.

Note: When preceded by the preposition "à." the forms of "lequel" contract with "à" to beacome "auquel." "à laquelle.""auxquels," and "auxquelles."
e.g., Le concert auquel il va → The concert to which he goes.

Quoi

"Quoi" is only used when talking about things. It is used most of the time to refer back to its antecedent if it has a vague sense like the words "rien." "ce." "chose," or "quelque chose." It means "what." It is used after a preposition.

e.g., Je sais de quoi il s'agit → I know what it is about.

À quoi ça sert? → What is it for?

Où

"Où" is used plus a form of "lequel" to introduce a relative clause referring to a place in order to avoid using a preposition. It means "where."

e.g., Voilà la maison où il habite → There is the house where he lives.

 Voilà la maison dans laquelle il habite → There is the house in which he lives.

Dont

"Dont" refers to people or things. It means "whose." "of which." "of whom," or "with." It is used to refer to a clause introduced by the preposition "de." A possessive adjective can't follow it instead, use an article.

e.g., Je t'ai parlé de la table? → Did I tell you about the table?
 La table dont je t'ai parlé → The table I told you about.
 Nous parlons de quelqu'un → We are talking about someone.
 La personne dont nous parlons → The person of which we are talking about.
 Je connais ses parents → I know her parents.
 La fille dont je connais les parents → The girl I know the parents.

Note: After any preposition other than "de," the relative pronoun is either "qui" for a person or "lequel" for an object. Also, when "de" is included in a word or expression, such as "près de," the relative pronoun used is "lequel."
e.g., Je parle à la fille. Elle s'apelle Marie → I am talking to the girl. She is called Marie.
 La fille à qui je parle s'appelle Marie → The girl I am talking to is called Marie.

Note: "dont" needs to be used even though in English its equivalent isn't used. If the subject of your sentence is a person, "dont" is most commonly translated as "whose." If it is an object, the best translation is "with."

Ce Dont

"Ce dont" can be used before expressions requiring the preposition "de" to replace the noun. It means "what."

e.g., Vous avez besoin de repos → You need to rest.

　　　Il sait ce dont vous avez besoin → He knows what you need.

Le vocabulaire des choses liées aux enfants
The vocabulary of things related to children

Un berceau	A crib
Un lit à barreaux	A cot bed
Un couffin	A Moses basket
Un hochet	A rattle
Une couche	A nappy
Une sucette	A dummy
Un jouet	A toy
Un doudou	A comforter
Une peluche	A cuddly toy
Une pousette	A pram / A pushchair
Une baby-sitter	A babysitter
Une poupée	A doll
Un caprice	A tantrum
Être gaté(e)	To be spoiled
Être sage	To be calm and quiet
Obéïr	To obey
Désobéïr	To disobey
Être espiègle / Être coquin	To be mischievous
Être vilain	To be naughty
Un biberon	A baby bottle
Du lait en poudre	Formula milk
Allaiter	To breastfeed

Plus sur les pronoms personnels accentués
More about disjunctive pronouns

What are they for?

They are used to refer back to a name which has already been mentioned or to people whose identity is obvious from the context. Most often, they are used in short answers without verbs, for emphasis, or for contrast with the subject pronouns.

The disjunctive pronouns

Moi	Me
Toi	You
Lui	Him
Elle	Her
Soi	Oneself
Nous	Us
Vous (p)	You
Eux (m/p)	Them
Elles (f/p)	Them

When to use them

<u>After a preposition</u>

e.g., Elle parle de lui → She talks about him.

> *Note: When the object of a preposition is a thing rather than a person, "y"*
> *or "en" must be used.*
> *e.g., Je pense aux examens → Je pense à eux → J'y pense.*
> *Je parle de ce livre → Je parle de lui → J'en parle.*

<u>After a comparison</u>
e.g., Elle est plus intelligente que lui → She is cleverer than him.

<u>Alone for emphasis,</u>
e.g., Qui est là? Moi → Who is there? Me.

<u>To add emphasis to a pronoun</u>
e.g., Moi, je fais la salade, toi la tarte → I do the salad, you do the tort.

<u>After "ne … que"</u>
e.g., Elle n'aime que lui → She only loves him.

<u>Part of a compound subject</u>
e.g., Pierre et lui irons au parc → Pierre and him will go to the park.

<u>In combination with "même"</u>
e.g., Je le ferai moi-même → I'll do it myself.

Le vocabulaire de l'école
Vocabulary of school

Le directeur	The headteacher
Le maître	A primary school teacher
La maîtresse	A primary school teacher
Le professeur	A professor
Un enseignant	A teacher
Un élève	A pupil
Un écolier	A school child (primary)
Enseigner	To teach
Apprendre	To learn
Apprendre par coeur	To learn by heart
Une salle de classe	A classroom
Un cours	A class / A lesson
Une leçon	A lesson
La récréation	The recreation
La cantine	The canteen
Un note	A grade / A mark
Des devoirs	Homework
Une punition	A punishment
Un cartable	A schoolbag
Un examen	An exam
Les vacances scolaire	School holiday
Un trimestre	A term
Une interrogation	A test

Un contrôle	A test
La crèche	The nursery
La maternelle	Preschool
L'école primaire	Primary school
Le collège	High school
Le lycée	Sixth form
L'école secondaire	Secondary school
L'université	The university
Le brevet des collèges	GCSE
Le bac à lauréat	A-levels
Une licence	A degree / A bachelor's degree
Un master	A masters degree
Un doctorat	A PhD
Un étudiant	A student
Une thèse	A thesis
Faire des études	To do studies
Un camarade / Un copain	A school friend
Une bourse	A grant

Les pronoms objet direct

The direct object pronouns

What is it?

A direct object pronoun will replace a noun that can answer the question "quoi" for a thing or "qui" for a person.

e.g., J'appelle Marc → Tu appelles qui? → Marc.
Je mange un gâteau → Tu manges quoi? → Un gâteau.

The direct object pronouns

Le / la / l' / les

The definite articles are used as a pronoun to refer back to either persons or things. They precede the conjugated form of the verb.

Pronoun	English	Gender / Numeral
Le	It / Him	Masculine singular
La	It / Her	Feminine singular
L'	It / Him / Her	Before "h" or vowels
Les	Them	Plural

e.g., Jean lit le livre → Jean lit quoi? → Le livre → Jean le lit.
Je vois Marie → Tu vois qui? → Marie → Je la vois.

> Note: There are used for more things.

98

The pronoun "y"
The pronoun "y" is used to refer back to a place, to avoid mentioning it again. It means "there." It precedes the conjugated form of the verb.

e.g., Je vais en France. Je vais en France aussi!
    Je vais en France. J'y vais aussi!

> *Note: It is used for more things.*

Le pronom "en"
The pronoun "en" is used to replace a phrase introduced by "de" in a prepositional sense ("de" or "d'") and in a partitive sense ("du," "de la," "de l'," and "des"). It means "of," "from," "about," or "some." It is used to replace "de" and what comes after, the rest of the sentence won't change. It precedes the conjugated form of the verb.

e.g., Nous venons de New York → Nous en venons.
    J'ai du pain → J'en ai.
    Elle parle de ce livre → Elle en parle.
    J'ai beaucoup de livres → J'en ai beaucoup.

> *Note: It can be used to replace verbs that require "de," as well as, expressions of quantity not introduced by "de," like "beaucoup de," "pas de," "trop de," "plusieur," "quelques," ...*

> *Note: "quelques" means "some," and it has to be followed by "uns" or "unes" according to the gender of the noun when you use "en."*
> *e.g., J'ai quelques amis → J'en ai quelques-uns.*
> *   J'ai quelques voitures → J'en ai quelques-unes.*

Le vocabulaire du bureau
The vocabulary of the office

Le bureau	The office / The desk
L'ordinateur	The computer
Le calendrier	Calendar
L'emploi du temps	Schedule
La pause	The break
La réunion	The meeting
Un dossier	A file
Une photocopieuse	A photocopier
Un fax	A fax machine
Un téléphone	A telephone
Une imprimante	A printer
Une déchiqueteuse	A shredder
Un scanner	A scanner
Une présentation	A presentation
Une clé USB	A USB stick
Un disque dur externe	A hard drive
Une corbeille à papier	A wastepaper bin
Un écran	A screen
Un tableau	A board
Un document	A document
Un clavier	A keyboard

Les pronoms COI et COD
The direct and indirect object pronouns

Direct object

A noun will have a direct object when it can answer the question "quoi" (what) for a thing or "qui" (who) for a person.

e.g., J'appelle Marc → Tu appelles qui? → Marc.
  Je mange un gâteau → Tu manges quoi? → Un gâteau.

Indirect object

A noun will have an indirect object when it can answer the question "à quoi" (to what) for a thing or "à qui" (to who) for a person. As a result, all the verbs followed by the preposition "à" will introduce a noun with an indirect object.

The COI and COD pronouns

"Me," "te," "nous," and "vous" precede the conjugated form of the verb. They can only replace a person. They can be "objet direct" as well as "object indirect."

Pronouns	English
Me / M'	(To) me
Te / T'	(To) you
Nous	(To) us
Vous	(To) you

e.g., Paul aime moi → Il aime qui? → Moi → Paul m'aime.
  Paul écoute Marie et moi → Il écoute qui? → Nous → Paul nous écoute.
  Paul donne le gâteau à toi → Il donne le gâteau à qui? → À toi → Paul te donne le gâteau.

The COI pronouns

"Lui" and "leur," precede the conjugated form of the verb. They can only replace a person and are only "indirect object."

Pronoun	English
Lui	To him / To her
Leur	To them

e.g., Paul écrit à Marie → Il écrit à qui? → À Marie → Paul lui écrit.

Paul parle à Pierre → Il parle à qui? → À Pierre → Paul lui parle.

Paul écrit à ses sœurs→ Il écrit à qui? → À ses sœurs→ Paul leur écrit.

Note: When you need to refer to a person or a thing with a direct object use "le, la, l', les."

Le vocabulaire des fournitures de bureau
The vocabulary of stationery

Un stylo	A pen
Un stylo-plume	A fountain pen
Une cartouche d'encre	An ink cartridge
Un crayon	A pencil
Un taille-crayon	A pencil sharpener
Une gomme	A rubber
Une règle	A ruler
Une effaceur	An eraser pen
Un crayon de couleur	A coloured pencil
Un feutre	A felt-tip pen
Un trombone	A paper clip
Une punaise	A drawing pin
Une calculatrice	A calculator
Une agrafeuse	A stapler
Une agrafe	A staple
Du tipp-ex / Du blanco	Some tipp-ex
Du scotch	Adhesive tape
Une paire de ciseaux	A pair of scissors
Le perforateur	A hole punch
Un surligneur	A highlighter
De la colle	Some glue
De la patafix	Some blu-tack
Un tampon	A stamp

Un marqueur / Un feutre indélébile	A marker pen
Un cahier	A notebook
Un bloc-notes	A notepad
Un classeur	A folder
Un intercalaire	A divider
Une pochette plastique	A plastic punched pocket
Un post-it	A post-it

La place des pronoms
Position of pronouns

In simple tenses

In simple tenses, like the present tense, the imperfect tense, the future simple…, the pronouns precede the conjugated verb.

e.g., Paul me donne le livre → Paul gives me the book.

In compound tenses

In compound tenses, like the perfect tense or others, the pronoun precedes the conjugated form of the auxiliary verb.

e.g., Paul m'a donné le livre → Paul gave me the book.

In a negative sentence

In a negative sentence, "ne" precedes the pronoun and "pas" follows the conjugated verb.

e.g., Paul ne me donne pas le livre → Paul doesn't give me the textbook.
    Paul ne m'a pas donné le livre → Paul didn't give me the book.

With an infinitive verb

When there is an infinitive verb in the sentence, the pronoun precedes the infinitive verb.

e.g., Paul veut me donner le gâteau → Paul wants to give me the cake.

Note: When an infinitive verb follows a verb of perception or the verb "laisser," the pronouns are placed before the conjugated verb and not before the infinitive verb.

e.g., Il me regarde faire la cuisine → He watches me cooking.

Je la laisse finir le travail → I let her finish the work.

With "voilà" and "voici"

The pronouns precede "voilà" and "voici."

e.g., Me voilà! → Here I am!

Double pronouns

When you refer back to a person or a thing with a direct or an indirect object, you can sometimes use two pronouns in the same sentences. In that case, you need to make sure that you follow the following rules.

Rules

	COI/COD	*COI*	*Definite*	*EN*	*Y*
COI/COD			Precede (e.g., 1)	Precede (e.g., 2)	Precede (e.g., 3)
COI				Precede (e.g., 4)	
Definite		Precede (e.g., 5)			
EN					
Y				Precede (e.g., 6)	

<u>Examples</u>

(1) Il me le donne → He gives it to me.

(2) Il m'en donne → He gives me some.

(3) Il nous y rencontre → He meets us there.

(4) Elle lui en donne → She gives him/her some.

(5) Il le lui donne → He gives it to him/her.

(6) Il y en a beaucoup → There are a lot.

Le vocabulaire des animaux de la ferme
The vocabulary of farm animals

Un canard	A duck
Un caneton	A duckling
Un mouton	A sheep
Une brebis	A ewe
Un agneau	A lamb
Un taureau	A bull
Une vache	A cow
Un veau	A calf
Un poney	A poney
Un âne	A donkey
Une anesse	A female donkey
Une chèvre	A goat
Un bouc	A billy goat
Un cochon	A pig
Une truie	A sow
Un porcelet	A piglet
Un coq	A cockerel
Une poule	A hen
Un poussin	A chick
Une oie	A goose
Une dinde	A turkey
Une pintade	A guinea fowl

Les verbes pronominaux et les différents temps
Pronominal verbs in the different tenses

Present

Affirmative sentence
Subject + reflexive pronoun + reflexive verb.

e.g., Je me réveille à 10 heures → I wake up at 10 am.

Negative sentence
Subject + ne + reflexive pronoun + reflexive verb + pas.

e.g., Je ne me réveille pas à 10 heures → I don't wake up at 10 am.

Present continuous

Affirmative sentence
Subject + "to be" in the present tense + en train de + reflexive pronoun + reflexive verb in the infinitive form.

e.g., Je suis en train de me réveiller → I am waking up.

Negative sentence
Subject + ne + "to be" in the present tense + pas + en train de + reflexive pronoun + reflexive verb in the infinitive form.

e.g., Je ne suis pas en train de me réveiller → I am not waking up.

Recent past

<u>Affirmative sentence</u>
Subject + "to come" in the present tense + de + reflexive pronoun + reflexive verb in the infinitive.

e.g., Je viens de me lever → I have just woken up.

<u>Negative sentence</u>
Subject + ne + "to come" in the present tense + pas + de + reflexive pronoun + reflexive verb in the infinitive.

e.g., Je ne viens pas de me lever → I haven't just woken up.

Imperfect

<u>Affirmative sentence</u>
Subject + reflexive pronoun + reflexive verb in the "imparfait"

e.g., Je me levais à 10 heures → I used to wake up at 10 am.

<u>Negative sentence</u>
Subject + ne + reflexive pronoun + reflexive verb in the "imparfait" + pas.

e.g., Je ne me levais pas à 10 heures → I didn't use to wake up at 10 am.

Perfect

<u>Affirmative sentence</u>
Subject + reflexive pronoun + "to be"in the present tense + reflexive verb's past participle.

e.g., Je me suis levé(e) à 10 heures → I woke up at 10 am.

Negative sentence

Subject + ne + reflexive pronoun + "to be" in the present tense + pas + reflexive verb's past participle.

e.g., Je ne me suis pas levé(e) à 10 heures → I didn't wake up at 10 am.

Near future

Affirmative sentence

Subject + "to go" in the present tense + reflexive pronoun + reflexive verb in the infinitive form.

e.g., Je vais me lever à 10 heures → I am going to wake up at 10 am.

Negative sentence

Subject + ne + "to go" in the present tense + pas + reflexive pronoun + reflexive verb in the infinitive form.

e.g., Je ne vais pas me lever à 10 heures → I am not going to wake up at 10 am.

Future simple

Affirmative sentence

Subject + reflexive pronoun + reflexive verb in the future simple.

e.g., Je me lèverai à 10 heures → I will wake up at 10 am.

Negative sentence

Subject + ne + reflexive pronoun + reflexive verb in the future simple + pas.

e.g., Je ne me lèverai pas à 10 heures → I will not wake up at 10 am.

Present conditional

<u>Affirmative sentence</u>
Subject + reflexive pronoun + reflexive verb in the conditional.

e.g., Je me lèverais à 10 heures → I would wake up at 10 am.

<u>Negative sentence</u>
Subject + ne + reflexive pronoun + reflexive verb in the conditional + pas.

e.g., Je ne me lèverais pas à 10 heures → I would not wake up at 10 am.

Les animaux de la savane et de la jungle
Animals from savana and jungle

Un singe	A monkey
Un lion	A lion
Un zébre	A zebra
Une girafe	A giraffe
Un éléphant	An elephant
Un crocodile	A crocodile
Un aligator	An alligator
Un gorilla	A gorilla
Un tigre	A tiger
Une chauve-souris	A bat
Un rhinocéros	A rhinoceros
Un hippopotame	A hippopotamus
Une gazelle	A gazelle
Un suricate	A meercat
Un léopard	A leopard
Un lynx	A lynx
Un perroquet	A parrot
Un buffle	A buffalo
Une antilope	An antelope
Une autruche	An ostrich
Un guépard	A cheetah
Un phacochère	A warthog
Un chacal	A jackal

Une hyène   A hyena

Note: The female of the lion is "une lionne."

L'impératif
The imperative

What is it?

The imperative is the form of a verb that is usually used for giving orders, commands, or instructions. Imperative is used to give instructions, like in the manual for examples, will not sound as direct as a command or an order.

How to form it?

The imperative can only be formed from the present tense of "tu," "nous," and "vous." The subjects "tu." "nous," or "vous" are never used for the imperative, only the conjugated form of the verb for these pronoun subjects is used.

e.g., Regardez! → Look!
   Assis-toi! → Sit down!

> *Note: Instead of using the imperative, the verb "devoir" can be used to give a command. It will sound as direct as the imperative.*
> *e.g., Arrête-toi! → Stop (yourself).*
>   *Tu dois t'arrêter! → You must stop (yourself).*

Affirmative imperatives

To use the imperative in an affirmative sentence, simply follow the rules explained above. When using the conjugation of "nous," it means "let's + verb."

e.g., Parle! → Speak!
   Attendons! → Let's wait!
   Finissez! → Finish!

Note: With "tu" you need to take off the final "s" at the end of the present tense of "-er" verbs.
e.g., Mange! → (Tu manges) → Eat!

Note: You can add "y" after an imperative to implicitly mean "there." Remember to add an "s" at the end of the imperative of "-er" verbs for 'tu' and make a "z" link.
e.g., Vas-y! → Go for it!
*   Allons-y → Let's go (there).*

Note: You can add "en" after an imperative to mean "of it" or "about it." Remember to add an "s" at the end of the imperative of "-er" verbs for "tu" and make a "z" link.
e.g., Parles-en! → Speak about it!

The affirmative imperative of reflexive verbs

The imperative of a reflexive verb can only be formed from the present tense for "tu," "nous," and "vous." The subjects "tu," "nous," or "vous" are never used for the imperative, only the conjugated form of the verb for these pronoun subjects is used. The reflexive pronoun follows the verb and is joined to it by a hyphen.

e.g., Habille-toi! → Get ready!
    Levons-nous! → Let's get up!
    Brossez-vous les dents! → Brush your teeth!

Note: The reflexive pronouns "te" or "t'" become "toi" in the imperative.
e.g., Lève-toi! → Get up!

The negative imperative

Place "ne" in front of the imperative form of the verb and "pas" after it.

e.g., Ne crie pas! → Don't shout!

Note: "ne" becomes "n'" in front of a vowel or "h."
e.g., N'abandonne pas! → Don't give up.

The negative imperative of reflexive verbs

When using the imperative form of a reflexive verb in a negative sentence, the reflexive pronoun will precede the verb.

e.g., Ne t'énerve pas! →Don't get upset!

The imperatives of "être," "avoir" and "savoir"

The imperative forms of "être," "avoir," and "savoir" are irregular. Instead of using the present tense, we use the subjunctive.

	Être	*Avoir*	*Savoir*
Tu	Sois	Aie	Sache
Nous	Soyons	Ayons	Sachons
Vous	Soyez	Ayez	Sachez

e.g., Soyez prêt à 10 heures ! → Be ready at/by 10 am!

Le vocabulaire des animaux marins
The vocabulary of marine animals

Une baleine	A whale
Un penguin	A penguin
Un dauphin	A dolphin
Un requin	A shark
Un crabe	A crab
Une étoile de mer	A starfish
Une pieuvre	An octopus
Une méduse	A jellyfish
Une otarie	A sea lion
Une orque	A killer whale
Une morse	A walrus
Un coquillage	A shell / A shellfish
Un hippocampe	A seahorse
Un calamar	A squid
Une raie	A ray
Une murène	A moray eel
Une anguille	An eel
Une moule	A mussel
Une anémone	An anemone
Une crevette	A prawn
Du corail	Coral
Une langouste	A rock lobster / A spiny lobster
Un homard	A lobster

Un oursin	A sea urchin
Un ours polaire	A polar bear

Les verbes "rater" et "manquer"
The verbs "to miss" and "to lack"

The verb "to lack"

In French, the verb "manquer" is used to translate "to lack" when you don't have enough of something or when you don't have something. The verb "manquer" needs to be followed by the preposition "de" and a noun, even when "of" is not used in the English sentence.

e.g., On manque d'informations → We lack information.
     Je manque de confiance en moi → I lack confidence in myself.

The verb "to miss"

In French, the verbs "manquer" and "rater" are used to translate "to miss."

<u>With an emotional meaning</u>
When the verb "to miss" is used in English with emotional meaning, for example, when you miss someone, the verb "manquer" is used in French. The construction of the sentence in French is different from what obtains in English. As a result, a literal translation from one language to another will not work.

e.g., Tu me manques → You miss me → You miss (to) me.
     Je te manque → I miss you → I miss (to) you.

The thing that is emotionally missed needs to start the French sentence. It can be a proper name, a pronoun subject, or an article and a noun. The person who misses that thing needs to follow it in the form of a COD or COI pronoun.

e.g., La France me manque → I miss France.
     La France manque à moi → France miss to me (litteral translation).

Note: Here, in the English sentence "I miss France," the thing that is emotionally missed is "France." "France" needs to start the French sentence. The person who misses "France" is "I." "I" needs to follow "France" and it has to be translated using a COD/COI pronoun. The French sentence is "la France me manque."

Note: Possessive adjectives can also be used as in English: in front of the "thing" that is missed.
e.g., Son fils lui manque → He/she misses his/her son.

Note: When the person who is missing the "thing" is not a personal subject pronoun, but it's a proper noun or a possessive adjective and a noun, the sentence's structure changes. The verb "manquer" has to be followed by the preposition "à." which will be followed by the person missing the "thing."
e.g., Nous manquons à mes parents → My parents miss us.
    Elle manque à son fils → Her son misses her.

Without an emotional meaning

When the verb "to miss" is used in English without an emotional meaning, for example, when you miss an appointment or an aeroplane, the verb "rater" is used in French.

e.g., J'ai raté mon rendez-vous! → I have missed my appointment!

Acknowledgement

I would like to thank my family and more particularly my husband for his support and help.

Isabelle and Nicky for their help with the proofreading.

My fellow French and English teacher friends for all our discussions about teaching.

My clients for their encouragement.

And all the people who have been my clients over the past five years for having helped me become the teacher I am today.

About the author

Hello,

I am Anaïs, an experienced and qualified native French teacher, passionate about teaching from an early age.

After my master's degree in education, I moved to England where I started to teach French as a foreign language to people of all levels, ages, and backgrounds. As my experience of learning English at school wasn't great, I decided to focus on creating an enjoyable way of learning French through dynamic, fun and rewarding lessons. During that time of teaching, I had the opportunity to create my own teaching materials, which follow a logical progression in learning the language, and I used them to write this book.

I always believe that my enthusiasm will benefit my students' learning as I am really a sociable, friendly and non-judgmental teacher. For me, teaching French is more than just a job, it's a passion. I see it as a mission, and this is why I dedicated my time completely to my students' learning journey. I am always enthusiastic, and I like to push my clients to exceed their expectations. I am a positive person, and I think that everything is doable with a bit of work, support, and goals to achieve along the way. I think that languages can be taught more effectively with interesting and fun lessons. In my opinion, learning French should never be boring!

I live in London, where I teach French in person or via Skype to people from different parts of the world.

For more information, please visit my website, www.anais.me.uk

"Learn French with Anaïs, as if you were having private lessons"
ISBN 9781717845887

Contact:
Anaïs Vella
www.anais.me.uk
hello@anais.me.uk

22312371R00072

Printed in Great Britain
by Amazon